THE CELESTIAL
Handbook

I'd like to give many thanks and love to my beloved family and friends, who have always encouraged me to shoot for the stars.

Illustrations by Catherine Rowe
Cover designed by Ana Bjezancevic
Typeset by Barbara Ward

This Ixia Press edition, first published in 2024, is a slightly modified republication of the work, originally published by Michael O'Mara Books Limited, London, in 2023. The text has been edited for an American audience.

ISBN-13: 978-0-486-85300-0
ISBN-10: 0-486-85300-4

IXIA PRESS
An imprint of Dover Publications

Manufactured in China
85300401   2024
www.doverpublications.com/ixiapress

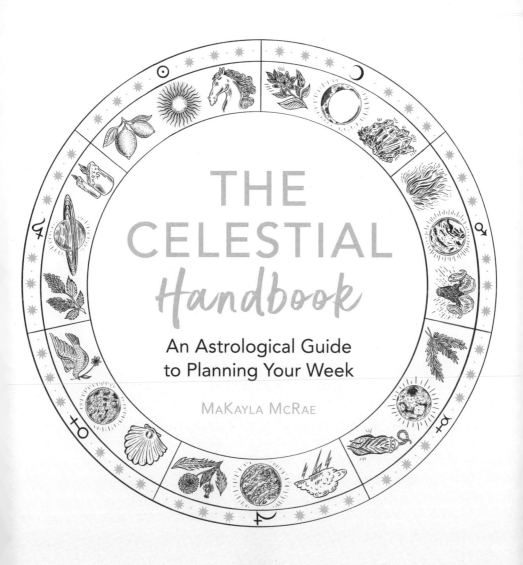

THE
CELESTIAL
Handbook

An Astrological Guide
to Planning Your Week

MaKayla McRae

ixia
PRESS

Garden City, New York

Contents

Introduction

Flowing with the current of cosmic energy, not against or in resistance to it, has the ability to change one's life. By planning in energetic alignment, your days, weeks, months and years move with more natural ease. Understanding the mysterious energetic forces that influence us individually and societally helps us move and plan with proper foresight.

With spiritual knowledge, you're more likely to know when it's time to assert yourself and take action versus when it's best to lean back, relax or observe. Since ancient times, people have looked to the sky for answers, divinity and guidance. Ancient astronomers were also astrologers, meaning the scientific and spiritual studies of the planets went hand in hand. These professional stargazers were responsible for naming the first major planets discovered in our solar system.

These planets had one thing in common: they were visible to the naked eye, at a time before telescopes and other technological advancements allowed us to peer into the vast depths of our universe. The planets were named after the ancients' god or goddess archetypes: Mercury, Mars, Venus, Jupiter and Saturn. And of course, what we now consider "the luminaries," the sun and moon, were recognized as planets. Each day of the week was assigned rulership in correlation with one of these seven traditional planets and deities, creating the planetary days. Starting with Sunday or Sun Day, the day of the sun, all the way to Saturday or Saturn Day, the day of Saturn, each planetary day has a vastly different energetic signature. Each influences the collective and personal efforts of humanity. By knowing the meaning behind these day-to-day shifts, we empower and redefine our lives.

Sunday

The first day of the week, Sunday, is, unsurprisingly, ruled by the sun. The radiant star is the center of our solar system, responsible for sustaining life for all living creatures on Earth. Without this giant force, we could not and would not exist.

In ancient Greece, the sun was associated with the god Apollo. They believed that he rode his golden chariot led by fiery horses across the sky at sunrise to bring light to the world below.

The sun rules our ego, identity and self-expression. It is the center of our being or life force, giving us fierce confidence. Our sun reminds us of the values that define us and the characteristics that we long to embody. Without its existence, life on Earth simply could not exist. Like humanity relies on the sun, we rely on our own inner solar energy to feel alive. Without its light, we can't spiritually "'see." We feel weary, weak and disheartened. With its light, darkness is illuminated. We feel capable, visible and mighty.

When we are not in alignment with sun energy, we feel the impacts loudly. We feel disconnected from our sense of self and may develop imposter syndrome. Our confidence is dimmed. We dismiss our values and needs and therefore forget what matters most to us, and what we need to feel alive and thriving.

On Sundays, we are encouraged to be ourselves loudly and proudly! It is time to focus on our creative talents, passion projects, self-development, illumination and discovery. When we follow this inner calling, we find much more success in our actions. It's true, however, that too much of a good thing can become a bad thing. Overconfidence works against our best interests just as much as insecurity does. Sunday is a day to avoid excessive hubris, pride or overzealousness. Remain grounded in your sense of self while keeping an open mind and the ability to listen, compromise and work with others.

On the first day of the week, plan with your passions in mind. Wearing your heart on your sleeve and following your creative whims brings about the most successful Sun Days. Making mistakes is human, but when we carry ourselves with self-assuredness we can bounce back from any challenge life throws our way. On this day, reconnect with the core of your being to build irreplaceable inner strength. Visiting theatrical, inspiring settings is ideal. If you get the chance to step into the spotlight, don't hold back! Being visible brings blessings. The sun doesn't ask for permission to shine.

Planning Sunday

Dos

- Be confident
- Show leadership
- Be creative
- Be direct
- Take action
- Perform
- Be independent
- Show positivity

Don'ts

- Be bossy
- Seek validation
- Be serious
- Put things off
- Be passive
- Be shy
- Isolate yourself
- Be negative

Sunday exercise: build your confidence

Prepare your space with music, fragrances and calm lighting to allow you to feel centered. Be sure to have a pen and paper nearby. When you have prepared your setting, take a few deep breaths and allow your body to relax.

1. When you have reached a focused state, set a ten-minute timer and begin to write a list of things that fill you with a sense of heightened self-confidence. The list can contain goals of things that you'd like to accomplish and would bring you pride.

2. What will you focus on? Perhaps past experiences that, when you recall them, make you feel assured of your abilities. Or a piece of music or a picture that lifts you up and connects you to a strong state of being.

3. Allow your scattered thoughts to fill up as much space as you can. By setting a timer, you challenge yourself to focus on the task at hand, write as much as you can and truly freely flow your thoughts rather than overthink.

4. When your time is up, reflect on your responses and dwell in the feeling of pride and possibility. Hopefully, this exercise reminds you that self-assuredness comes from dwelling on the good already within you. Choose some points you'd like to focus on for the next four Sundays. You may choose to celebrate a past accomplishment by treating yourself on one Sunday. The next Sunday, you may choose to dedicate time to map out one of your inspiring goals. By intentionally aligning your actions with the energy on the day of the sun, you allow yourself to attract more success and wins that will bring gratification and joy.

Sunday ritual: supercharge

In this ritual you'll charge yourself with the light and power of the sun. Sunlight holds powerful, illuminating, energizing spiritual vibrations. Many of us believe that when we spend a day outside tanning, we feel and look like we are glowing. Just by sitting in sunlight, you can intentionally welcome solar beams to further help you glow up in a spiritual sense.

All this ritual requires is this simple intention and focus as you bask in beams for a few minutes. You may choose to include your energy tools for an additional boost, such as sun-ruled crystals like sunstone or quartz (see the chapter on energy tools for more ideas).

As you bask in the sunlight, close your eyes and ask the universe to grant you courage, confidence and whatever other solar qualities you think would promote your healing journey. When you've finished, thank yourself for taking the time to show up for yourself.

Mantras

A positive mind attracts
positive outcomes.

✦

Each decision, big or small, brings me
closer to or further from my higher self.

✦

Any step in the right direction is
progress, no matter how small.

✦

I am capable of making miracle shifts in
my life by being authentically myself.

✦

I will stand true to my self-expression,
regardless of external perceptions.

Monday

Mondays, or "Moon Days," are ruled by the moon. Waxing and waning, this celestial body is ever-changing, just like our emotions. Mythologically, we associate the moon with the ancient Greek goddess Artemis, goddess of the moon and the hunt. She asked her father, Zeus, to permit her to live an eternally chaste lifestyle. She dedicated her time to embodying the responsible role of protector of women, nature and animals. Her fierce, independent personality, coupled with her sensitive desire to protect, allowed her to live introspectively, passionately and according to her own moral cues.

Astrologically, the moon relates to our truest emotions. The moon represents our sense of home, security and nostalgia.

Alignment with lunar energy feels like being present with our current reality while paying homage to our past and roots. It is the experience of knowing we can trust our gut and following through without feeling the need to explain our logic to others.

However, any unbalanced lunar energy can result in withdrawing into ourselves to an extreme, avoiding vulnerability, or merging with others' emotions to the point we struggle to identify or stand within our own convictions and identity. Oversensitivity can leave one drained, trying to find a deeper meaning in everything.

On Moon Days, we are asked to get in tune with our innermost feelings and to listen to our sensitivities. On this day, we honor our feminine energy, regardless of gender, and lean into the power of our psychic foresight to lead us to what matters most to us. It is a day to avoid emotional extremes such as oversensitivity and to embrace moving slow but steady. Hosting events in your home, private spaces and gatherings with loved ones also prove ideal.

Planning Monday

Dos

- Intuit -
- Feel -
- Be compassionate -
- Respect your roots -
- Slow down, rest -
- Be present -
- Be independent -
- Spend time with family -

Don'ts

- Gaslight yourself -
- Be moody -
- Neglect yourself -
- Forget to be present -
- Lack boundaries -
- Burn out -
- Forget your roots -
- Be materialistic -

Monday exercise: writing

Automatic writing is the art of channeling the answers to your inquiries. You can ask for guidance from your guides, angels, higher self or whatever sense of higher power you connect to. This exercise may come to you naturally, but don't be discouraged if it doesn't come to you with ease on the first try. This exercise may require repetitive practice over the course of a few Moon Days. Write down your burning question at the top of a blank page. Simply set the intention to allow the answer to come through.

1. Then free-flow write, without stopping to think at all. Let both cohesive and jumbled thoughts alike come through. Words, sketches, full sentences, feelings and more are welcome.

2. You may decide to set a timer to help you focus on getting as much written as time permits, rather than overthink and block channeling from

coming through. Or you can simply write until you feel you have fulfilled your need.

Optional: when completed, pull a Tarot or oracle card for further divine clarity on your message.

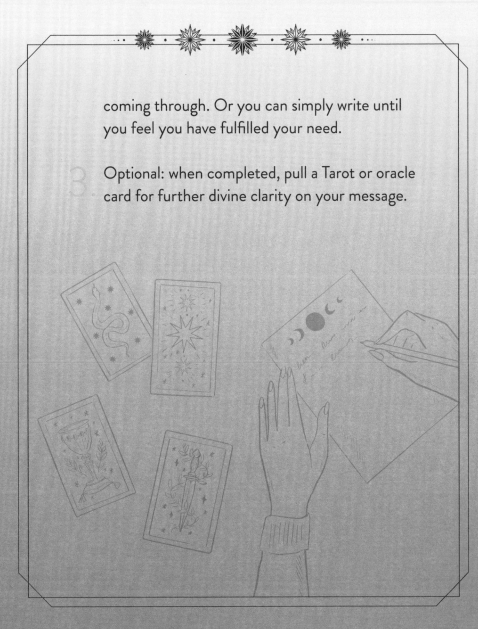

Monday ritual: crystals

Charge your crystals under the luminous light of the moon on a Moon Day to keep, carry and utilize the energy of the mystical luminary with you at any time. A moonstone or selenite crystal is especially helpful, as these stones are already attuned to the energy of the moon (see the energy tools chapter for tools you may choose to use). Any phase of the moon will suit your magical needs to replenish, recenter and reconnect with your heart. If a new or full moon happens to fall on a Moon Day, performing this ritual will yield extra-potent results. You may choose to sit under the radiant yet subtle beams as well. If not, leave your crystals outdoors to bask in the lunar vibes and bring them back in before sunrise.

Mantras

I will listen to my inner compass rather than base my decisions on what others tell me.

✦

I move instinctively and intuitively. What my mind cannot solve, my soul has already known.

✦

My intuition will never steer me in the wrong direction when I listen.

✦

My innermost feelings and sensitivities are not a weakness; they are messengers to guide me.

✦

I extend the same compassion I give freely to others to myself.

Tuesday

‧‧ ✦ ‧‧

Tuesdays are associated with Mars. The fourth planet from the sun is visible from our view on Earth on occasion, its red glow commanding attention in the night sky. In Greco-Roman mythology, Mars was the war god, known for his impulsive, dominant, bold and brash nature. However, there were many other myths that portrayed Mars as the warrior who delivered much-needed justice. Anger can be quite a motivating, freeing force. It lets us know when we need to say no, set a boundary, get space or assert our free will in a more constructive direction. Mars teaches us that we don't always have to silence our voices to avoid rocking the boat or to keep the peace.

Mars represents our sexuality, passion, self-preservation, energy levels and vitality. It's no surprise that the ancient divine feminine force and the goddess of love, Venus, took Mars as her secret lover. While Venus' domain of love, romance, bliss, attraction and harmony are sacred forces of nature, so is Mars' dualistic mirror of autonomy, sexuality, self-respect, survival and protection.

Mars' energy teaches us to embrace passion, willpower, boundaries and healthy confrontation. Unchecked intensity, recklessness and unnecessary aggression hinder us.

Mars is key for healthy masculinity and expression, regardless of our gender. We can change the world when we feel we can assert our needs and protect our fellow warriors fighting through life. "I'm a lover not a fighter, but I fight for what I love" encapsulates the purpose of an aligned Mars expression.

On Tuesdays, make your passionate urges a priority and your self-respect law. Get in tune with your inner warrior and use frustration, anger or tensions as positive motivators to break free from limiting circumstances. Question what you tolerate and ensure proper boundaries. Avoid sweeping what bothers you under the rug by courageously confronting issues. Sporting events, athletic pursuits and games are ideal affairs to attend.

Planning Tuesday

Dos

- Keep active
- Assert yourself
- Be direct
- Take action

- Be honest
- Set boundaries
- Pep talks
- Build yourself up

Don'ts

- Laziness
- Aggression
- Procrastination
- Lack tact

- Harshness
- Fighting
- Power games
- Tear others down

Tuesday exercise: move your body

Mars rules physical movement, so on Tuesday, plan to get your body actively in alignment with your mind and spirit. When we neglect our physical body, we dismiss and neglect a core part of our needs. A great way to utilize Mars Day is by taking a meditation walk to help regulate your nervous system and energy levels.

During a meditation walk, the goal is to silence your mind by being as present and grounded as possible with the sensations you feel as they arise in your body.

2. How does the ground feel beneath your feet with each step? How does the temperature feel on your skin? Where does your body feel relief as you pace? How fast or slow are you walking? How much is that connected to your state of mind? Where are you experiencing emotions in your body, and how can you bring loving attention to your emotional state by caring for that area? (See the chakras chapter for the body's energy centers and their spiritual needs.)

3. How do you feel before and after your walk? What kind of thoughts arise?

4. After you finish, sit and take a moment to pause. Think of where you noticed tension or unease in your body. Take a moment to visualize yourself breathing in white, cleansing light to that area. Breathing out, visualize dark light leaving, relieving you of any negativity.

Tuesday ritual: light a candle

Mars rules both fire and the color red, so what ritual could be more perfect than burning a red candle on a Mars day?

1. On a Tuesday, sit down in a calm environment, close your eyes and visualize that you are breathing in red, passionate, invigorating and motivating light.

2. When you exhale, visualize that dark, negative or stagnant light is leaving your body to make more space for the inspiration you are calling in. Breathe in to the count of 7, hold your breath for 6 and breathe out for 8. Repeat for a few minutes, until you feel in flow.

3. When you are ready, open your eyes, light your candle and give thanks to yourself and the universe for cultivating and heightening your Mars energy.

4. Over the course of a week, until the next Mars Day, notice if any inspired actions or intuitive insights come to you surrounding self-preservation, advocacy, growth and Mars archetypal themes. Be sure to jot down musings as they come. Plan to put them into fierce action either to inspire autonomy or to call more assertive, active growth into your life.

Mantras

I believe my needs are worth advocating for.

✦

I honor my fluctuating energy levels; I find
ways to stay on track or motivated on my
good, bad and in-between days.

✦

I believe it is not mean or wrong to exercise
my right to say no.

✦

My boundaries are worth honoring.

✦

I plan and take actions to fulfill, rather than
just passively long for, my desires and goals.

Chakras

Chakras are energy centers located within our bodies, running from the top to bottom of the spine. In Sanskrit, chakra translates to "wheel," which perfectly conveys how chakras move, spinning in a wheel-like motion. The chakras can either spin too slowly, at just the right speed in balance or too fast. Our relationship to each energy center in our body and its associations will determine how healthily it can function. There are seven main chakras, aligning with the classical seven planets and their associated seven planetary days of the week. Balanced chakras yield a healthy relationship to our physical body and good health, as well as spiritual, emotional and mental alignment.

Sunday

The Heart Chakra is the sun's chakra and is associated with Sun Days. Astrologically, the sun rules your physical heart, so this connection is quite literal.

Location: Center of chest

Color: Green

Purpose: Emotions acting as divine messengers and prompting guidance; compassion; subjectively finding what matters most for joy and fulfillment

Balanced: Experiences heartfelt truth that transcends language; open to life; self-love; care for others

Unbalanced: Lacking love or compassion for self or others; emotionally repressed; hypersensitive; shallow or hurried breathing; poor circulation

Ways to Balance: Being present with emotions as they ebb and flow; identifying feelings and how they feel in the chest; sunbathing

Monday

The Third Eye Chakra is the moon's chakra and is naturally associated with Moon Days. Astrologically, the moon rules your eyes and eyesight. Consequently, the Moon Chakra is correlated to this spiritual-sighted chakra.

Location: Forehead, slightly above and between the eyebrows

Color: Indigo

Purpose: Bridges the unconscious and conscious mind; deep inner wisdom and intuition; nonphysical and physical vision

Balanced: Trusting our intuitive judgment; pattern recognition; foresight; perceives energy beyond material vision; receptive to divine communication, omens and signs

Unbalanced: Distrust in future; limited listening and comprehension disconnected from spirituality; headaches

Ways to Balance: Building a relationship with your intuition via dream journaling and interpretation; visualizing breathing in indigo light into the third eye; placing crystals on your third eye during meditation or a prayer to the universe

Tuesday

The Solar Plexus Chakra is Mars' chakra and is associated with Mars Days. Astrologically, Mars rules your physical energy and vitality, so the connection to the chakra of motivation is clear.

Location: The "core," the stomach area below the ribs

Color: Yellow

Purpose: Instincts; gut feeling; energy in the body; personal power; willpower; self-confidence

Balanced: Trust in one's worth and value; decisive; self-motivated; purposeful; strong and confronts challenges

Unbalanced: Insecurity; indecisive; gives personal power away; hides from hardships; aggressive or passive-aggressive; paranoid; fatigue; restless

Ways to Balance: Sitting with anger and frustration as it arises; boundaries or redirection; sitting by a fire; physical activity; walking meditations

Wednesday

Mercury's chakra is associated with the Throat Chakra and Mercury Day. It's no surprise that Mercury astrologically rules the throat. It is also correlated with the nervous system, making the Throat Chakra our processing center as we perceive and internalize external stimuli.

Location: Center of the neck

Color: Blue

Purpose: Speaking one's truth; listening; understanding; conveying inner wisdom; perception

Balanced: Direct communication; clear voice; aware; strong observational skills; steady learner

Unbalanced: Passive communication; passive-aggressive; limiting self-expression; sore throat; hearing difficulties; difficulty learning and retaining information

Ways to Balance: Meditation to clear away the mental chatter that drowns out your authentic inner voice; journaling; developing healthy communication skills

Thidsday

Located at the top of the head is the Crown Chakra. This is Jupiter's chakra and is associated with Jupiter Days. Astrologically, Jupiter rules prophecy and spirituality, which correlates with the chakra of higher connection.

Location: Top of the head

Color: Violet

Purpose: Connects one to the universe, higher power, all that is; bird's-eye view of life; universal consciousness

Balanced: Feeling connected to life; living versus surviving; positive attitude; peaceful; trust in the universe; trust in divine timing

Unbalanced: Apathy; confusion; spiritually lost; cynical attitude; existential; distrust of self and life; insomnia

Ways to Balance: Praying or giving offerings to one's higher self or higher power; giving to others or to charity; practicing gratitude

Friday

Venus' chakra is associated with the Sacral Chakra and with Venus Day. Astrologically, Venus rules pleasure, so it is naturally associated with the chakra of enjoyment, sexuality and emotional fulfillment.

Location: Below the navel

Color: Orange

Purpose: Creativity; life force; joy; pleasure; fantasy; warmth; connecting with others

Balanced: Inspired; finds positivity; openhearted; friendly; charming disposition; sexually liberated

Unbalanced: Creatively blocked; finds negativity; too serious and calculated; detached disposition; sexually repressed or hypersexual; relationship problems

Ways to Balance: Swimming, floating or bathing in a body of warm water; treating yourself to a fun experience; physical touch and intimacy; allowing yourself to practice vulnerability and be present in relationships

Saturday

Saturn's chakra is associated with the Root Chakra and with Saturn Day. Astrologically, Saturn rules one's lower body, which correlates with the Root Chakra's placement at the base of the spine.

Location: Base of the spine

Color: Red

Purpose: Foundation of self and life; stability; link to the material realm and Earth

Balanced: Feeling safe and reliable with yourself and the environment; basic needs met; care for your physical body

Unbalanced: Ungrounded; lacking healthy routines and structure; neglectful of the needs of self or others

Ways to Balance: Organizing your schedule; home; routines; diet; being in nature

Wednesday

Wednesdays are our hopeful hump day that promises that we are halfway through the workweek. At this point, we are settled into our weekly habits and are in a more productive headspace. Wednesdays are associated with the clever messenger of the ancient Greco-Roman gods, Mercury. The deity was known for his sneaky, cheeky, trickster personality.

Mercury may be the smallest planet in our solar system, but it also holds the title of being the closest planet to the sun. With the sun representing both our literal and spiritual life force, this meant Mercury's close position to the giant star must hold some significant spiritual meaning. And therefore, assigning the planet to the god who relayed messages for the king of all gods was only fair.

Mercury represents one's communication and intellectual skills. The way we process information, actively listen, absorb external stimuli, engage in conversation, learn and interpret with our intellect are all connected to Mercurial energy. Through the influence of Mercury we make space for learning, education, communication, our local community, relaying information and problem-solving.

This archetype allows us to use our head over our heart. Healthy communication habits are encouraged to ensure that we can speak our mind and understand with intention and clarity. Unbalanced Mercury expressions can cause us to bite our tongue, communicate untruthfully, avoid hard truths or struggle to fully listen with the intention to understand. Mental scatteredness, indecisiveness and overthinking hold us back from the calculated, mental clarity that our Mercury energy can bless us with.

Be sure to communicate and check sources directly. College, higher education, libraries, bookstores and academic settings or ideas are ideal environments for this day.

Planning Wednesday

Dos

- Listen to understand
- Bring people together
- Fact-check
- Be flexible
- Learn new things
- Be productive
- Communicate kindly
- Analyze

Don'ts

- Say too much
- Gossip
- Jump to conclusions
- Have comfort zones
- Be pretentious
- Act without intention
- Avoid truth
- Assume

Wednesday exercise: happy talk

1. On Wednesday, try to set the intention to have three or more uplifting and helpful verbal exchanges. As the saying goes in most things magic- and manifestation-related: all good things come in threes!

Whether you compliment a stranger on their outfit, ask for clarification when your coworker's directions confuse you or set boundaries with someone who is talking down to you, seek to use communication as the powerful tool it is. Speak your mind.

3. At the end of the day, reflect on your communication on this Mercury Day. Where did your communication habits help you? Hinder you? What will you try again? What would you do differently next time?

4. If you feel called to, journal your reflections to keep tabs on your progress throughout your communication journey.

Wednesday ritual: express yourself

Take a piece of paper or record yourself speaking aloud, free-flowing thoughts you've been holding in. Going for a walk or drive sometimes helps you in this practice. Maybe there is something you wish you could have said to someone, or maybe you have been trying to resolve an ongoing personal problem. Perhaps you just need a general mental reset by venting about anything and everything. When you feel you have expressed your thoughts as fully as possible, feel free to light a gray candle; diffuse rosemary, cardamom or peppermint essential oils; or utilize any Mercury energy tool (see the energy tools chapter) to further welcome in heightened, evolved and mentally clear Mercurial energy.

Mantras

I don't have to and shouldn't believe every
thought that enters my head.

✦

The answer isn't to sharpen my heart but
my mind.

✦

When I stop problem-solving and be present,
I flow in tune with divine timing.

✦

I act with the truth that my voice is worthy
of healthy expression.

✦

I am mindful that my communication habits
can either greatly help or hinder my journey.

The Day You Were Born

If you were born on a Sunday

Those who were born on a Sunday are known for their passionate and bold approach to life. Leadership comes naturally to them, or, at the very least, they are not afraid to be the first to take risks that entail following their heart. Even if they are more reserved, sun personalities cannot help but shine and be noticed. Striving for personal empowerment, those born on a Sun Day may come off as blunt, direct or stubborn to some. However, they are just sure of what they want out of life and don't wish to waste time settling for less. They are called to lead a life of authenticity, getting to know how to remain in tune with their ever-evolving self and identity.

If you were born on a Monday

Those who were born on a Monday are intuitive and empathetic, and they effortlessly bring a sense of home and comfort to others. Monday children are often cool, calm and somewhat mysterious to others on first impression. However, they are the caretakers of the seven days-of-the-week archetypes, investing their heart and soul into loved ones and protecting the innocent. They are very easygoing and only become agitated or aggressive when someone tries to harm someone they love.

These individuals must be especially mindful of the company they keep, as they wear their hearts on their sleeves. Their loving nature often leaves them easily influenced by others' emotions, energy and needs, whether they care to admit their sensitivity or not. They are called to develop their psychic abilities and prioritize their inner compasses.

If you were born on a Tuesday

Those who were born on a Tuesday are headstrong, calculated and individualistic. They are called to learn to live a life in alignment with their true, core desires and passions rather than settle for external validation. Some may feel that their nature is rather intense, but they often try to create spaces where everyone around them feels comfortable enough to be their true selves by being unapologetically authentic by example. It is important for a Mars person to find an outlet for their high energy by remaining active, through sports or other physical activities. Otherwise, they run the risk of feeling disconnected from their fast-paced, intuitive nature or become easily agitated and anxious.

If you were born on a Wednesday

Those born on a Wednesday are intellectually motivated. They are chatty by nature with those who make them feel comfortable. When they are not feeling their best, they tend to go to the other extreme and fall noticeably quiet. These people are called to treat life like a school of evolution and growth. Silencing their voice, being cynical about change and avoiding the fluidity that life asks of them leaves them feeling drained, scattered and powerless. When they seek to learn from their experiences, open their mind to new perspectives and communicate their unique takes with others, life flows with more ease.

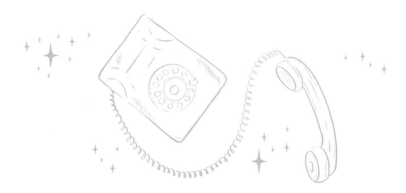

If you were born on a Thursday

Those born on a Thursday are philosophical, optimistic and often fortunate. When they claim their confidence, their presence is immediately noticed when they walk into any room. However, their present-minded approach to life sometimes makes them miss out on important details when planning for the future, leading them into sticky situations. Luckily, they are rather lucky! Solutions often come naturally, even if put together at the last minute. Thursday folk are frequently asked to get out of their comfort zone to experience all they can in their lifetime. They feel stuck when they limit themselves to one lifestyle or philosophy for too long. When they experiment, rather than get caught up in one perspective, they attract abundance, resources and good energy.

If you were born on a Friday

Those born on a Friday are known to be hopeless (or hopeful!) romantics, loving love and prioritizing the magic that can only arise from human connection. These individuals know how to see beauty in almost everything and everyone. Because of this optimistic perspective, they are often artistically motivated and inspired. However, their rose-tinted glasses outlook can leave them blindsided at times when they find that many others see the world and relationships in a different light. They are called to dedicate their sacred time and energy to partners, friends and chosen family who align with their refined values and commitments.

If you were born on a Saturday

Those born on a Saturday are known to be dedicated, refined and committed. These individuals have a strong moral compass and feel it's everyone's responsibility to make the world a better place by doing their part. Because of this characteristic, they are often very serious about their goals and sense of purpose. However, they must be thoughtful and remain open-minded about how their ideas of what's right or wrong may differ from others' values. They are called to live a life of integrity and make decisions based on their responsibility to give themselves a full, balanced life.

Thursday

Jupiter, the planet associated with luck, expansion and growth, rules Thursday. This makes Thursday quite a high vibration day, where luck is often high and confidence soars. Jupiter is the largest planet in our solar system and the fifth planet from our sun.

The Greco-Roman god Jupiter was the most powerful force to exist in the heavens. Gods, goddesses and humans alike had to obey commands from the king of the gods.

Jupiter's marriage to the goddess Hera didn't stop him from going after what and whom he wanted. In fact, most of the ancient deities were fathered by him. Being the embodiment of mightiness, impressiveness and authoritativeness, it was Jupiter's world and everybody else was just living in it.

Jupiter represents luck, fortune, success, enthusiasm and ambition. Harnessing our Jupiter energy in its glory makes us magnetic and our very own lucky charm. On this day, we focus on empowering ourselves with wealth, luck, success, happiness, harvests and celebration. Remember that you are deserving of whatever you need to feel expansive, so long as it causes no harm to you or others.

On Jupiter day, we ponder the question: "What if I just had the audacity and faith to do what I truly wanted?" The downside is that risk management and humility can be lacking within Jupiter's realm. Jovian energy fuels people with a sense of confidence, but we must be careful not to fall into arrogance or a lack of humility and respect for those around us.

On Thursdays, travel, fun, leadership and calculated leaps of faith are highly encouraged. But forgetting your limitations and responsibilities? Not so much. Channel confidence as it is more readily available. Take leadership of your life's direction on this very auspicious day. Avoid any extremes of self-importance, and remain mindful of your moral and social obligations to those around you. If others become bossy or self-righteous, remember to pause before reacting. Luxury, extravagance, culture, spiritual places of worship and international settings are all ideal on a Jupiter day.

Planning Thursday

Dos

Take calculated risks   Be grateful

Be confident   Travel

Show leadership   Self-care

Manifest your goals   Spiritually recenter

Don'ts

Act indestructible   Be selfish

Show hubris   Have comfort zones

Be overbearing   Be preachy

Downplay your potential   Be narrow-minded

Thursday exercise: vision board

1. Prepare your space, and set the intention to create a vision board to call in your higher self and life. A vision board is where you collect imagery that gives you a representation of what you want to manifest or create and experience in your life.

2. You may choose to make one digitally through creating a board online on Pinterest, pinning images that you feel represent your dream day. You can use magazine clippings to create art on a poster that reflects your heart's calling. Printing aesthetic photos can help.

3. When you have gathered your materials, actual or virtual, put your full focus on your vision board. Bask in the feelings these images would bring if they were to become your reality.

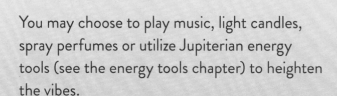

You may choose to play music, light candles, spray perfumes or utilize Jupiterian energy tools (see the energy tools chapter) to heighten the vibes.

4. Going forward, adding to, modifying or simply basking in your vision board on Jupiter days will aid in manifesting the most successful results.

Thursday ritual: new adventures

On Thursday, plan to take a trip that you have not had before. This could be as simple as walking a few minutes away to a place in your neighborhood you have never walked to or as elaborate as going on a trip to a foreign land. Taking in your surroundings, leave a simple Jovian offering (see the energy tools chapter) to the land around you, and set the intention that this charm will attract more abundance into your life, even when you return home.

This simple adventure acts as a ritual because it shows the universe that you are ready to make the time and effort to explore new experiences and mental shifts to welcome in the abundance you desire. Taking the first step to get out of your comfort zone and regular routine creates an energetic space for the universe to introduce you to more of the expansion you seek to manifest.

Mantras

Miracles follow me.

＋

When I'm grateful for what I have, the
universe can bless me with more.

＋

My wildest dreams are on the other side of
calculated risk.

＋

What I want wants me more.

＋

I believe that I'm lucky and things always
work out for me.

Energy Tools

Energy tools are objects, symbols, concepts and overall "things" that we can utilize to tap into the energy of the different planetary archetypes. For example, on Sunday, using solar-ruled energetic tools can boost your luck even further and assist in executing your day's plans more successfully. On Monday, using lunar-ruled energetic tools boosts luck, and so on and so forth.

Energy tools allow us to realign with the more positive expressions of a planetary archetype and to neutralize its more negative dimensions. These tools amplify intentions and heighten rituals, or they can simply act as reminders. You may choose to carry these items, wear them or place them on your spiritual altar or sacred space. Energy tools are healing, spiritual remedies.

Sunday (Sun) energy tools

The items listed below carry signature solar energy as well as strength and illumination. They are to be perceived radiantly and cover all the sun's domains.

Sunday energy tools include: sunstone, quartz crystal, orange essential oil, lemon essential oil, the color yellow, yellow candles, turmeric (herb), hawks

Monday (Moon) energy tools

The items listed here carry signature lunar energy support: emotional healing, heightened intuition, psychic awareness, divine femininity, peaceful domestic life, nurturance and generating feelings of emotional security. They cover all of the moon's domains.

Monday energy tools include: moonstone, selenite, white rose petals, jasmine essential oil, the color white, white candles, mugwort (herb), rose water, deer

Tuesday (Mars) energy tools

The items listed below carry signature Martian energy: embodying passion, courage and taking autonomous leadership. They cover all of Mars' domains.

Tuesday energy tools include: red jasper, carnelian, coffee, the color red, red candles, musky fragrances, ginger essential oil, black pepper essential oil, cayenne (herb), boars, rams

Wednesday (Mercury) energy tools

The items listed here carry signature Mercurial energy: embodying clear expression, communication and heightened intellectual abilities. They cover all of Mercury's domains.

Wednesday energy tools include: fluorite, the color gray, gray candles, rosemary essential oil, cardamom essential oil, peppermint (herb), rabbits, snakes

Thursday (Jupiter) energy tools

The items listed here carry signature Jovian energy: creating an auspicious aura and ensuring success. They cover all of Jupiter's domains.

Thursday energy tools include: amethyst, tigereye, the color purple, purple candles, sandalwood essential oil, clove essential oil, dandelion (herb), eagles

Friday (Venus) energy tools

The items listed below carry signature Venusian energy: embodying love, beauty, sensuality, self-love and relationship healing. They cover all of Venus' domains.

Friday energy tools include: rose quartz, lapis lazuli, emerald, pearls, rose petals, the color pink, the color violet, pastel colors, pink candles, sweet fragrances, rose essential oil, lavender essential oil, vanilla perfume, yarrow (herb), daffodils, daisies, doves, seashells, cherubs, cherries

Saturday (Saturn) energy tools

The items listed here carry signature Saturnian energy: addressing adulthood needs, organizing efficiently and thinking long-term.

Saturday energy tools include: obsidian, onyx, the color brown, brown candles, patchouli essential oil, pine essential oil, Saint-John's-wort (herb), owls

Friday

Friday is associated with Venus, the goddess of love, allure, attraction and beauty. All things pleasurable, enticing and heartfelt are under her domain. The Greco-Roman goddess Venus was the most charming, sensual, seductive force of nature to exist. Desirability was her magnetic superpower.

The second planet from the sun, also known as "Earth's twin," the planet Venus was associated with the ancients' revered goddess of love. Why? Similar to their goddess's eye-catching beauty, the radiance of Venus twinkles beautifully and is the brightest of all in the night sky. This planet has mysterious, magnetic energy, influencing us to become more aware of the power of persuasion and desire.

Venus is our love language, how we showcase and receive love. Venus shows us the type of love we idealize and long for, both platonically and romantically.

Venus also encourages us to exercise moderation as the planet of balance and harmony. We must control excessive urges to reach for pleasure and desire; otherwise, we are at risk of being controlled by our superficial impulses and lose sight of true happiness and contentment. Venus seeks justice, peace and connection with others but knows the importance of self-care and self-love.

On Fridays, be light, romantic, kind and relationship-oriented. It's time to appreciate the artistic vision in everything and anything. Take it easy with work and heavy labor. Relax. Create when inspiration strikes. However, find the fine line between uplifting optimism and ignoring your better judgment.

Don't let desires blind you to the point of unhealthy jealousy or possessiveness. What is meant for you will be for you. Planning a romantic date or bringing some TLC to your relationships goes a long way. Going to art exhibitions, artistic events and concerts, and being pampered can prove especially delightful.

Planning Friday

Dos

- Give and receive care
- Flirt
- Have fun
- Love yourself

- Socialize
- Enjoy the arts
- Pamper yourself
- Be romantic

Don'ts

- Close your heart
- Mislead
- Be serious
- Ignore red flags

- Neglect yourself
- Rush
- Be insecure
- Demand work

Friday exercise: wish list

This is a simple four-step writing exercise that helps you proactively manifest your dream lover, friend or companion.

1. On a fresh piece of paper, write down a list of qualities and traits that you desire to find in the lover, friend or companion you're seeking. Get as detailed as possible, and don't be afraid to write even the most seemingly obvious characteristics. For example, if you want a long-term relationship, make sure you include that you'd like your dream lover to be single and emotionally available.

2. Underline the qualities that you already embody or are a part of your everyday life. For example, you desire a friend to do workouts with and you already spend time working out.

3. Next, circle the traits you do not embody. For example: you desire an adventurous partner but often decline opportunities to get out of your comfort zone and be adventurous, or you desire a friend who thinks positively but are often thinking or speaking negatively.

4. Looking at your circled traits, plan a goal or task that can help you develop this quality within yourself. By taking action, you create energetic space to call forth your ideal companion. For example, plan a spontaneous vacation with a friend or a solo trip to a restaurant you've always wanted to try in order to attract your adventurous partner.

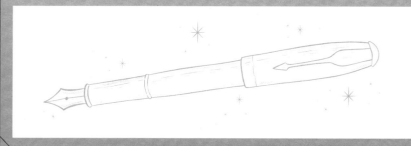

Friday ritual: attracting love

1. Take an empty glass jar, and put in a bit of honey.

2. Then either place a photo of yourself or a piece of paper with your name written on it into the jar. Put in more honey, and seal the jar.

On top, burn a candle and allow the wax to drip over, sealing it shut. You may choose to first anoint this candle with a Venusian essential oil, such as rose or lavender, and then roll in yarrow, a Venusian herb, to heighten Friday's potential energy (see the energy tools chapter).

When you have finished, call in self-love, beauty, romance, attraction, allure, loveliness, balanced relationships and connections through affirmation: "Love surrounds me now."

Mantras

Self-love is the secret ingredient to attracting what I deserve.

When I flirt with life, life flirts back.

The answer is to sharpen my mind, not my heart.

I stop and smell the roses.

I find pleasure, fun and romance within my current means; I do not need to wait and long for the "right" circumstances to find happiness.

Tarot

Tarot is a tool for divination that allows one to tap into universal truths. A Tarot deck consists of seventy-eight cards, which fall into two categories: the Major and Minor Arcana. The majority of the deck belongs to the Minor Arcana, consisting of fifty-six cards. This category covers everyday life events, feelings or details. "Minor Arcana" roughly translates to "little secrets." These cards represent what is easily accessible, in our free will and conscious control.

Twenty-two cards hold significant interpretations and speak of vital archetypal themes, known as the Major Arcana. "Major Arcana" roughly translates to "big secrets," relating to major life lessons, experiences or mysteries. The Major Arcana represents fated and karmic times.

By understanding which of the Major Arcana archetypes corresponds to each day of the week, we gain insight into the esoteric knowledge, power and lessons that each day holds.

Sunday

THE SUN

Enlightenment

Joy

Celebration

The Sun card denotes that a period of darkness is coming to an end. We have gone through the muck and mud of our problems to gain more clarity on who we are and what we need for ourselves. On Sun Day, we are asked to be light-hearted. Even if we are in a strange life chapter, it's a good time to celebrate our progress, reflect on how far we have come and be gentle with our inner child. Being optimistic will attract good opportunities and luck like a magnet.

Monday

THE HIGH PRIESTESS

Inner knowing

Spiritual vision

Trusting your intuition

Subconscious mind

On Mondays, we are urged to follow our gut feelings. Feelings are messengers in disguise. Our body often becomes more sensitive to negative energy intentions the more that we heal. Be sure to keep track of your dreams on the morning or following day of a Moon Day night as well. Messages from ethereal realms are more likely to come through.

Tuesday

THE EMPEROR

Independent decision-making

Leadership

Mind over matter

Self-discipline

Tuesday's Tarot reading: we are in charge of our lives. The appearance of the Emperor reminds us that each decision we make, big or small, comes with real consequences. The Emperor is ready to take his full share of responsibility and doesn't fear the potential of his full power unlocked. We are urged to reclaim our power on Mars Day. At any given moment in time, we have the power to make new decisions, say no to what's draining us, and reprioritize and restrategize.

Wednesday

THE MAGICIAN

Willpower

Focused efforts

Making it happen

Mastering your craft

Learning

On Mercury Day, our mental state matters. Reminding ourselves to feed our mind with good thoughts and to challenge negative beliefs as they arise is important. In order to manifest desired external results, a seed must be planted internally. The media we consume, conversations we have, self-talk we engage in and things we spend lots of time thinking about will take us closer to or further away from the reality we seek. Consciousness is your key.

Thursday

WHEEL OF FORTUNE

Change

Repeating cycles
or breaking patterns

Fortune

Luck

On Jupiter Day, stay aware, alert and present to find great opportunities that you can further explore and expand upon. The Wheel of Fortune speaks of luck on both ends of the spectrum – good or bad luck. If we're to block ourselves off and remain in our comfort zone, we may feel unlucky from our own interference. Be bold and follow through on the matters calling to your soul.

Friday

Living with an open heart

Remaining grounded

Sensuality

Relationship healing

Effortless magnetism

On Venus Day, we are called to reconnect to the power of the Empress. She reminds us that empowerment doesn't always need to come from a place of being demanding. When we are healed, centered and at peace within ourselves, our presence alone radiates warmth and draws in attention. Set your standards high. People may want access to you and your time, energy, warmth and comfort, but is it pulling you away from your peace of mind?

Saturday

THE WORLD

Completion

Graduation from cycles and lessons

Full circle moment

Ideal outcomes from long-term strategizing paying off

On this day, it's important to think with the end in mind. Every day we are tempted to fall into impulsivity, reactivity or fleeting temptations. Perhaps someone you're dating is giving you half their heart, but you want something serious. Or you are accepting a job offer out of fear that something better won't come along. With the World, we are reminded that Saturn Days are to treat our time like the prized commodity it is. Time is money, and how we spend it matters.

Saturday

On the final day of the week, we enter the realm of Saturn. Being the sixth planet from our sun, the planet is known for its captivating rings and orbiting moons. In ancient Greco-Roman times, Saturn was regarded as the king of all gods once upon a time. He embodied relentless rulership, partaking in cruel actions because his power went unchecked. That was before his son Jupiter overthrew him.

Saturn reminds us that long-lasting things take months or years to form. We must take responsibility for our power in how we direct and spend our time. Things that come from a hurried or ego-based approach often aren't built to survive the unpredictable highs and lows in life.

Saturn represents our restrictions, boundaries, limitations, karma and maturity. In this spiritual realm, rules are defined and breaking them results in fair, predictable consequences. Morals are of utmost importance. Slowing down and focusing on what matters most ensures we reap the Saturnian rewards of wisdom, success and long-term happiness.

Saturn teaches us that we must say no to the things that do not align with our future aims. We only have so much time and energy. However, being too strict can cut us off from our loving, vulnerable, fun-loving human nature. Someone who is too rigid is arguably at a loss, just as much as someone who doesn't plan or set boundaries at all. Balance is key.

On Saturdays, tackle challenges. Complete tasks you've been putting off and dedicate time to constructive means. We all get tempted to veer off the path of our code of ethics from time to time, but Saturday is the day to avoid slipping up. Any settings that allow you to focus, step into authority or have a structured system for you to follow are ideal.

Planning Saturday

Dos

- Focus
- Be mature
- Take responsibility
- Put in the effort
- Be ethical
- Have patience
- Connect to traditions
- Ground yourself

Don'ts

- Procrastinate
- Avoid integrity
- Avoid accountability
- Neglect your heart
- Harshly judge others
- Resist change
- Neglect individuality
- Be cynical

Saturday exercise: goal setting

This exercise aids you in planning for the present while keeping your big picture interests in mind.

1. On Saturn Day, write down a list of tasks that you want to accomplish in both the short term and long term. Think and write as much as you see fit; long or short lists work equally well.

2. Then break the list down into a realistic, manageable to-do list by categorizing the list into four headings: A: get done today; B: within ten days; C: within a month; D: within years.

3. By organizing your efforts you'll be better able to show up for your Saturn Days with efficiency, be able to work in the present and be prepared while keeping the long term in mind with each action you take.

4. Going forward, whenever you are feeling overwhelmed, scattered or confused, revisit this list as a reminder of what matters most and what isn't worth your time or energy.

Saturday ritual: grounding

Go outdoors and find a spot where you can get barefoot comfortably. This ritual is known as grounding, a healing practice that allows one to reconnect to the magical and spiritual properties of Mother Earth.

You may choose to hold onyx or obsidian crystals or wear Saturnian essential oils to welcome in healing energy (see the energy tools chapter).

Let your bare feet touch the earth. Breathing in, ground yourself by imagining roots growing from the ground, up into your feet and bringing you closer to nature like a tree. Allow all the tensions of your mind, body and spirit to go down through the roots and back to natural sources.

When you are ready, open your eyes and thank yourself for your presence. Repeat this exercise any Saturday to end your week and prep for the next on a secure note.

Mantras

I am capable and ready to act with
responsibility for myself and my future.

+

My future can be predicted by my
daily routines.

+

I will put in the extra effort to live
the life I dream of.

+

Accountability frees me from illusions.

+

I honor my upbringing, traditions and
history while holding space for discovering
my own principles, morals and beliefs.

Summary

The planetary days are an ancient practice that allow us to redefine how we live out the days of the week in our modern-day lives. Utilizing the planetary days starts by understanding the archetypal energy of the planet associated with each day and keeping it in mind as you make everyday decisions. Reclaiming our power by aligning our daily routines and plans within the cosmic astrological flow, we find more peace, ease, love, success and abundance. The following resources allow you to have an integrated understanding and practical guides to use for future reference.

The chart on the next page is a quick reference to recall the key points of each planetary day for accessible, convenient planning.

The planetary days cheat sheet

Day	Planetary ruler
Sunday	Sun – ego, individuality among others
Monday	Moon – emotions, reflective of others
Tuesday	Mars – action, passion, energy
Wednesday	Mercury – communication
Thursday	Jupiter – power, success, luck
Friday	Venus – love, relationships, beauty
Saturday	Saturn – structure, responsibility

The planetary ruler section explains the energy of the day, the chakras allow you to heal and center, and the keywords summarize how to set intentions and plan your daily goals.

Chakra	Keywords to embrace
Heart Chakra	Boldness, creativity, spotlight, talent
Third Eye Chakra	Intuition, nurturing, community
Solar Plexus Chakra	Assertiveness, direction, initiative
Throat Chakra	Articulate, question, explain, listen
Crown Chakra	Confidence, leadership, celebrate
Sacral Chakra	Fun, pleasure, enjoy, relax
Root Chakra	Organize, define, stabilize, secure

Weekly celestial planning: What do you *wish* or *want* to experience this week for your own enjoyment or development?

1. What is *necessary* to put on your to-do list this week or has to get done?

2. Refer to the planetary days cheat sheet or the day chapters to refresh your knowledge.

3. Finally, organize your week's tasks or goals under the appropriate planetary day to ensure you succeed in expectations. Welcome to the magic of cosmic, foolproof planning!

Putting plans in motion

Below is a blank chart that can be copied and reused an infinite number of times as a weekly template to plan in synchronicity or flow with the planetary days:

Sun Day/Sunday

Moon Day/Monday

Mars Day/Tuesday

Mercury Day/Wednesday

Jupiter Day/Thursday

Venus Day/Friday

Saturn Day/Saturday

About the author

MaKayla McRae is an astrologer, Tarot reader and spiritual practitioner. As seen in *Vogue*, HypeBae, Bustle and other major publications, she has read for hundreds upon hundreds of individuals. Her clients range from the general public to notable celebrities and public figures. Born to a spiritually gifted family, she has been generationally raised to be in touch with and communicate her intuitive insight. You can keep tabs on her current projects and offerings via thestarryeyedmystic.com.

About the artist

Catherine Rowe is a British designer whose work embodies luxury. Inspired largely by her love of nature and wildlife, Catherine's illustrations marry tradition with contemporary style. She won the Liberty Open Call for a new iconic Liberty fabric in 2018. Her winning design, "Palace Gardens," was launched in 2019, and her career has flourished ever since. Catherine trained as an illustrator at Cambridge School of Art.
Visit catherinerowedesigns.com.